THE BLESSING

A Devotional of Bible Verses, Quotes and Affirmations

THE BLESSING

**A Devotional of Bible Verses,
Quotes and Affirmations**

TROY BARNES

RIGHT SIDE PUBLISHING
JOHN 21:6

Copyright

tbarnes2432@gmail.com

ISBN- 9781955050210

LCCN-2025914995

Published by

Right Side Publishing

P.O Box 339

Reynoldsburg, Ohio 43068

Printed in the United States of America

Editor: Felicia S. Cauley

Editor-Namra Malik

Cover design by- Shahin

Interior Design by- Shahin

Table of Contents

Introduction

The Blessing is an empowerment to prosper in every area of our lives given to us as an inheritance through our faith in Jesus Christ (Genesis 3:13-14). It's not just saying "bless you" when you hear someone sneeze, or a term used to express sympathy. It's meant to uplift, encourage, and strengthen in all areas of life. The more knowledge you gain of the real blessing Christ's death on the cross has provided mankind, the more you begin to walk in it. (2 Peter 1:2-4). And here is the good news (Gospel): it's available to all who believe (Romans 1:16). Throughout this devotional, you will see scriptures, quotes, and affirmations that highlight what Christ did for all who believe- examples of God's **Amazing Grace**, where all you need to do is **Just Believe and Don't perform**.

The Blessing

Genesis 12:2 NIV

"I will make you a great nation; I will bless you and make your name great; And you shall be a blessing."

Numbers 6:24-26 NIV

"The Lord bless you and keep you; the Lord make his face shine on you and be gracious to you; the Lord turn his face toward you and give you peace."

Affirmation – Father, I thank you for giving me the gift to bless people, empowering them through your word and your love. Thank you for your grace over my life, in Jesus' name, Amen.

The Power of Gratitude

Psalms 106:1 – "Praise the Lord. Give thanks to the Lord, for he is good; and his love endures forever."

3 Ways Gratitude Boosts Faith – Boosts are like taking spiritual vitamins!

- **<u>*Gratitude teaches us to enjoy "present" moments*</u>**. When we focus on what we're thankful for right now, we become more present and aware of God's goodness today. *"This is the day the Lord has made. We will rejoice and be glad in it." (Psalm 118:24 NLT)*

- **<u>*Gratitude delivers peace when combined with prayer.*</u>** *Don't worry about anything; instead, pray for everything. Tell God what you need and thank him for all he has done. Then you will experience God's peace, which exceeds* *anything we can understand. His peace will guard your hearts and minds as you live in Christ Jesus. (Philippians 4:4-7 NLT)*

- ***Gratitude brings enough.*** When we thank God, we're reminded that He has already promised to meet all our needs through Christ's abundance. *"And the God who takes care of me will supply all your needs from his glorious riches, which have been given to us in Christ Jesus." (Philippians 4:19 NLT)*

Affirmation – Father, I thank you for this day, I will rejoice and be glad in it. I thank you that I'm blessed to be a blessing to others today in Jesus' name. Amen!

Love is Required

1 John 4:11 NLT _Dear friends or Beloved, since God loved us that much, we surely ought to love each other._

1 John 4:19 NLT _We love each other, because he first loved us._

Romans 5:5 NLT _And this hope will not lead to disappointment. For we know how dearly God loves us, because he has given us the Holy Spirit to fill our hearts with his love._

The Most Important Commandment

Matthew 22:37-40 _Jesus replied, "You must love the Lord your God with all your heart, all your soul and all your mind. This is the first and greatest commandment. A second is equally important: Love your neighbor as yourself. The entire law and all_ *the demands of the prophets are based on these two commandments.*

John 13:34 - *So now I am giving you a new commandment: Love each other. Just as I have loved you, you should love each other.*

1 Corinthians 13:13 – *These three things remain: faith, hope, and love. But the greatest of these is LOVE.*

Love transforms us into people who reflect more of the character of Jesus Christ.

Paul was saying to the Corinthians that no one can remain the same after encountering God's love.

Faith is the key to Christianity, as it is what saves us. Hope is what we place in God that he will keep his promises. Love is not just what God does; it is who He is. And His love will remain forever.

Highest Form of Love = Agape - Fatherly love of God for us and human reciprocal love for God.

"Abba Father" (Abba is Greek for father)

Romans 8:15 *So you have not received a spirit that makes you fearful slaves, instead you received God's spirit when he adopted you as his own children. Now we can call him Abba, Father. For his spirit joins with our spirit to affirm that we are God's children, we are his heirs, in fact, together with Christ, we are heirs of God's glory.*

Galatians 4:6-7 *- And because we are his children, God has sent the spirit of his Son into our hearts, prompting us to call out "Abba, Father! Now you are no longer a slave but God's own child. And since you are his child, God has made you, his heir.*

1 Corinthians 13:4 *- Love is patient and kind. Love is not jealous, boastful, proud, or rude. It does not demand its own way. It is not irritable, and it keeps no record about injustice but rejoices whenever truth wins out. Love never gives up, never loses faith, is always hopeful, and endures through every circumstance.)*

John 13:34 *- So now I am giving you a new commandment: Love each other. Just as I have loved you, you should love each other.*

Romans 8:37 *"In all these things we are more than conquerors through Him that loved us.*

Love is a GREAT TRANSFORMER.... LOVE transforms:

Ambition into Aspiration

Greed into Gratitude

Selfishness into Service

Getting into Giving

Demands into Dedication

Loneliness into Happiness

Affirmation – *Father, I thank you for loving me and giving me the ability to love others. I can love because you first loved me. Help me to spread love today. In Jesus' name, Amen.*

Spiritual Pairing or Connection

<u>Romans 8:15 and Galatians 4:6-7</u> - *His spirit joins with our spirit to affirm we are God's children, sent his spirit into our hearts.*

<u>Romans 10:10</u> – *For it is by believing in your heart that you are made right with God, and it is by confessing with your mouth that you are saved.*

<u>Romans 10:11-13 NLT</u> – *As the scriptures tell us, "Anyone who trusts in him will never be disgraced. Jew and Gentile are the same in this respect. They have the same Lord, who gives generously to all who call on him. For everyone who calls on the name of the Lord will be saved."*

<u>Affirmation</u> – *Father, I thank you for loving me and giving me the ability to love others. I can love because you first love me. Help me to spread that love. In Jesus' name, Amen!*

Power of Your Words

Proverbs 18:21 NLT – *The tongue can bring death and life; those who love to talk will reap it the consequences.*

Proverbs 6:2 NKV – *You are snared by the words of your mouth; you are taken by the words of your mouth.*

Matthew 12:34 – *For out of the abundance of the heart the mouth speaks. Or whatever is in your heart that's what your mouth will say.*

1 Peter 3:10 *"For he that will love life, and see good days, let him refrain his tongue from evil, and his lips that they speak no guile.*

<u>Affirmation</u> – _Father, I thank you for giving me the ability to speak life and not death, blessings and not cursing, love and not hate. Help me to speak and spread your good news in Jesus' name, Amen!_

> **Receive Christ, Receive His spirit.
> He moves in!**

- ***1 John 4:13 NLT*** – *And God has given us his Spirit as proof that we live in him and he in us.*

- ***1 John 4:16-19 NLT*** – *We know how much God loves us, and we have put our trust in his love. God is love, and all who live in love, live in God, and God lives in them...as we live in God, our love grows more perfect...we will not be afraid on the day of judgment, but we can face him with confidence because we live like Jesus here in this world.*

- ***2 Corinthians 5:17 NLT*** – *This means that anyone who belongs to Christ has become a new person. The old life is gone; a new life has begun.*

- **_2 Corinthians 5:18 NLT_** – *And all of this is a gift from God, who brought us back to himself through Christ. And God has given us this task of reconciling people to him.*

- **_2 Corinthians 5:19 NLT_** – *For God was in Christ, reconciling the world to himself, no longer counting people's sins against them. And he gave us this wonderful message of reconciliation.*

- **_Reconciliation_** - *means the act of restoring a relationship or making two things compatible again.*

- **_2 Corinthians 5:20 NLT_** – *So we are Christ's ambassadors; God is making his appeal through us. We speak for Christ when we plead, "Come back to God!"*

- **_2 Corinthians 5:21 NLT_** – *For God made Christ, who never sinned, to be the offering for our sin, so that we could be made right with God through Christ.*

Affirmation– *Father, I thank you for moving into my heart and giving me the ability to reconcile others back to you! In Jesus' name, Amen!*

Abraham Justified by FAITH.

- **Romans 4:1,2 and 3 -** *What then shall we say that Abraham, our forefather according to the flesh, discovered in this matter? If, in fact, Abraham was justified by works, he had something to boast about-but not before God. What does the scripture say? "Abraham believed God, and it was credited (or accounted) to him as righteousness."*

- **Romans 4:4 and 5 -** *Now to the one who works, wages are not credited as a gift (or grace) but as an obligation. However, to the one who does not work but trusts God who justifies the ungodly, their faith is credited (or accounted) as righteousness.*

- **Romans 4:6** – *David says the same thing when he speaks of the blessedness of the one to whom God credits righteousness apart from works:*

- ***<u>Romans 4:</u>7*** – *Blessed are those whose transgressions are forgiven, whose sins are covered.*

- ***<u>Romans 4:8</u>*** – *Blessed is the one whose sin the Lord will never count against them. (**<u>Paul is quoting David says in</u> <u>Psalms 32:1 NIV - "Oh, what joy for those whose disobedience (or transgressions) is forgiven, whose sin is put out of sight (or does not count against them)."</u>***

- ***<u>Galatians 3:29 -</u>*** *And if you are in Christ, then you are Abraham's seed (or offspring or true children), heirs according to the promise.*

<u>Message - God wants us to be free so we can spread the gospel of Jesus Christ EVERYWHERE WE GO!!</u>

<u>Affirmation - Father,</u> *I thank you, I have been justified by faith and not by my works or behavior. I thank you; I am Abraham's seed and an heir according to your promise. In Jesus' name, Amen!*

> **Abraham was justified by FAITH and credited with RIGHTEOUSNESS.**

- **_Matthew 6:33 -_** _Seek ye first the kingdom of God and HIS righteousness and all these things will be added to you."_

- **_Galatians 3:6 -_** _So Abraham believed God, and it was credited to him as righteousness._

- **_Galatians 3:7 -_** _Understand, then, that those who have faith are children of Abraham. Scripture foresaw that God would justify the Gentiles (non-Jews) by faith and announced the gospel to Abraham: "All nations will be blessed through you." **(From Genesis 17)**_

- **_Galatians 3:9, 10 -_** _So those who rely on faith are blessed along with Abraham, the man of faith. For all who rely on the works of the law_ are under a curse, as it is written: "Cursed is everyone who does not continue to do everything written in the Book of the Law. "(**Also, Galatians 1:8**)

- **Galatians 3:11 and 12 -** Clearly, no one who relies on the law is justified before God, because "the righteous will live by faith." The law is not based on faith; on the contrary, it says, "The person who does these things will live by them."

- **Galatians 3:13 and 14 -** Christ has redeemed us (or rescued us) from the curse of the law by becoming a curse for us, for it is written: "Cursed is everyone who hangs on a tree." He redeemed us so that the **BLESSING OF ABRAHAM** might come to the Gentiles (non-Jews) through Christ Jesus, so that by faith we might receive the promise of the Spirit.

- **Galatians 3:29 -** And if you are in Christ, then you are Abraham's seed (or offspring or true children), heirs according to the promise.

Affirmation– *Father, I thank you for the abundance of grace and the gift of righteousness given to me through my belief in Christ. In Jesus' name, Amen!*

⌐ NO CONDEMNATION. ¬

- ***Romans 8: 1 and 2 NLT*** So *now there is no condemnation for those who belong to Christ Jesus. And because you belong to him, the power of the life-giving Spirit has freed you from the power of sin that leads to death.*

- Condemnation – Root word is to "Condemn," which means to declare wrong, or evil, pronounce guilty, or tear down.

- Conviction – This is when the Holy Spirit reveals a specific area of sin (such as pride, jealousy, anger, lust, lying, or selfishness) that we need to confess and turn away from. Conviction draws us closer to God, leading us to His grace and forgiveness.

- **_John 3:17_** _For God did NOT send his Son into the world to condemn the world, but to save the world through him!_

- **_Romans 8:3 and 4 NLT_** _The law of Moses was unable to save us because of the weakness of our sinful nature. So, God did what the law could not do. He sent his own son in a body like the bodies we sinners have. And in that body God declared an end to sin's control over us by giving his Son as a sacrifice for our sins. He did this so that the just requirement of the law would be fully satisfied for us, who no longer follow our sinful nature but instead follow the spirit._

- **_Romans 8:34 NLT_** _Who then will condemn us? No one – for Christ Jesus died for us and was raised to life for us. He is sitting in the place of honor at God's right hand, pleading for us._ **_(Also 1 John 2:1-2 says we have an advocate)_**

- **_Romans 6:1 and 2 NLT_** _Well then, should we keep on sinning so that God can show us more_ *and more of his wonderful grace? Of course not! Since we have died to sin, how can we continue to live in it. "*

- ***Romans 6:14 NLT*** *Sin is no longer your master (or have dominion over you) for you no longer live under the requirements of the law. Instead, you live under the freedom of God's grace (his unmerited, undeserving favor).*

- ***2 Corinthians 5:21 NLT*** *– For God made Christ, who never sinned, to be the offering for our sin, so that we could be made right with God (or the righteousness of God) through Christ.*

Affirmation– Father, I thank you for the gift of no condemnation because of what Christ has done for me. Thank you that I am forgiven and can be free in Jesus' name, Amen!

YOU HAVE ACCESS

- **_Romans 5:1 and 2 NLT_** *Therefore, since we have been made right in God's sight by faith, we have peace with God because of what Jesus Christ our Lord has done. Because of our faith, Christ has brought us into this place of undeserved privilege (grace or unmerited favor) where we now stand, and we confidently and joyfully look forward to sharing God's glory.*

- **_Romans 5:3, 4 and 5_** *We can rejoice, too, when we run into problems and trials, for we know that they help us develop endurance. And endurance develops strength of character, and character strengthens our confident hope of salvation. And this hope will not lead to disappointment. For we know how dearly God loves us, because he has given us the Holy Spirit to fill our hearts with his love.*

- **_Romans 8:15 and Galatians 4:6-7_** - *His spirit joins with our spirit to affirm we are God's children, sent his spirit into our hearts.*

Affirmation - *Father, I thank you for the access I've been given through Christ. Because of Him, I stand in your grace and can call you, my Father. In Jesus' name, Amen!*

Faith of the Son of God

- **_Galatians 2:20 -_** _I'm crucified with Christ, nevertheless I live but Christ lives in me (takes up residence) and now I live by the faith of the Son of God._

- **_Romans 1:17, Galatians 3:11 and Hebrews 10:38_** _The just shall live by **_FAITH_**!_

- **_Romans 10:10_** _For it is with your heart that you believe and are justified, and it is with your mouth that you profess your faith and are saved._

- **_Romans 10:17_** _Faith comes by hearing, and hearing by the word of God._

Affirmation - *Father, I thank you for the faith I have through Christ to help me with my everyday needs. I thank you for this in Jesus' name, Amen!*

Heart and Mouth connection

- **<u>2 Corinthians 4:13 -</u>** *We have the same spirit of faith as our heavenly Father.*

- **<u>Proverbs 18:21</u>** *Life and Death is in the power of the tongue.*

- **<u>Proverbs 6:2</u>** *We're snared by the words of our mouth.*

- **<u>Matthew 12:34</u>** *Out of the abundance of our heart the mouth speaks.*

- **<u>Hebrews 4:14 and Hebrews 2:17</u>** *Jesus is the high priest of our confession. Merciful and Faithful high priest.*

- ***Hebrews 4:16***   *Let us come BOLDY unto the throne of GRACE, that we may obtain mercy, and find grace to help in a time of need.*

- ***Numbers 25-28***   *A symbolic head of the current priestly administration.*

- *In the law of Moses, the high priest would intercede on behalf of the people, bringing sacrifices repeatedly as the law prescribed.*

- ***Hebrews 2:17 and Romans 8:34*** *Jesus became our sacrifice by what he did on the cross. As a result, became our high priest and intercedes on our behalf even today.*

- ***1 John 2:1-2*** *He's, our advocate.*

- ***1 Peter 5:6 and 7. Also Philippians 4:6-7*** *Go to God in Prayer.*

- **_Psalms 148:1-6_**   *Giving him Thanksgiving and Praise Psalms.*

- **_1 Peter 4:10-11_** *Use your gift to serve others.*

Affirmation– Father, I thank you for the power of words that You have placed in my heart—words that praise Christ's love. Help me to use them to speak truth and share the blessing of Christ with others. In Jesus' name, Amen.

WE BELIEVE AND THEREFORE WE SPEAK

- **_2 Corinthians 4:13 -_** *It is written: "I believed; therefore, I have spoken." Since we have that same spirit of faith, we believe and therefore we speak.*

- **_Ephesians 1:3_** – *Blessed be the God and Father of our Lord Jesus Christ who **"has"** blessed us with all spiritual blessings in heavenly places in Christ.*

- He has already blessed us! He gave you the root to all the fruit. Christ in YOU

- Spiritual blessing is in heavenly places, and heavenly places are in Christ, and Christ is in you.

- You are currently walking around with every-thing you need on the inside of YOU!

- The more exposure you have to God's word on grace (His unmerited, undeserved favor) and what Jesus has done for you, it will get into your heart. Grace is the person of Jesus Christ and all He has done.

- **_Romans 5:17_** *NLT - For the sin of this one man, Adam, caused death to rule over many. But even greater is God's wonderful grace and his gift of righteousness, for all who receive it will live in triumph over sin and death through one man, Jesus Christ.*

- **_Matthew 9:20-22 ASV -_** *And behold, a woman, who had an issue of blood twelve years, came behind him, and touched the border (or hymn) of his garment: for she* **_said within herself, I shall be made whole._**

- **_Matthew 8:5-13 -_** *The centurion said,* **_"Speak the Word"_** *and my servant will be healed.*

- **_Psalms 27:13 -_** _David says, "**I will see the goodness of the Lord in the land of the living**. Wait for the Lord; be strong and take heart and wait for the Lord."_

- **_Romans 10:10_** _For it is with your heart that you believe and are justified, and it is with your mouth that you profess your faith and are saved._

- **_Matthew 12:34_** _Out of the abundance of our heart the mouth speaks._

- **_Proverbs 18:21_** _Life and Death is in the power of the tongue._

- **_Proverbs 6:2_** _We're snared by the words of our mouth._

Affirmation– Father, I thank you for loving me and giving me the ability to speak your word over every situation in my life. I thank you that I can expect to see and experience your goodness in all things. Help me to spread this goodness. In Jesus' name, Amen!

GRACE – UNMERITED FAVOR OF GOD

- **2 Peter 1:2 -** *Grace and Peace be multiplied unto you through the knowledge of God and of Jesus our Lord. NLT says, "May God give you more and more grace and peace as you grow in your knowledge of God and Jesus our Lord."*

- NIV translation is "Grace and Peace be yours in ABUNDANCE."

- **2Peter 1:3 NLT** *By his divine power, God has given us everything we need for living a godly like. We have received all of this by coming to know him, the one who called us to himself by means of his marvelous glory and excellence.* **This is the Finished Works of Jesus Christ.**

- When we strive to know God and to learn what Christ taught while on earth, this is when grace and peace are multiplied to us.

> ## How do you experience God's grace and peace?

- *Learning what Christ taught and what was taught about him.* **Matthew 6:33**

- *By depending on his provision for each day.* **Philippians 4:6-7 also 19**

- *Having his intervention in situations that are difficult or impossible for you. There will never be a day you don't need God's grace.* **John 16:33**

- **John 1:16 -** *The law was given by Moses, but grace and truth came through Jesus Christ.*

- **_Isaiah 30:18 –_** _God longs to be gracious to us._

- **_Psalms 5:12 -_** _God favor surrounds us like a shield._

- **_Luke 2:52 -_** _Jesus had wisdom statue and favor with God and man._

- **_Ephesians 2:8-9_** _For by grace you have been saved through faith._

- **_2 Corinthians 12:9-10_** _His grace is sufficient for you; his power is made perfect in weakness._

- **_Hebrews 4:16_** _Boldly approach the throne of grace, that you will find help in a time of need._

- **_2Peter 1:3 NLT_** _By his divine power, God has given us everything we need for living a godly life. We have received all of this by coming to know him, the one who called us to himself by means of his marvelous glory and excellence._

- Peter is saying no one who knows God through faith in Jesus is missing anything we need to lead the godly life to which we are called. By the grace of God, all who trust in Christ have been made partakers in God's nature and purpose. This is our INHERITANCE, and we are sons of God.

- *__1 John 3:1__ See what kind of love the Father has given to us, that we should be called children of God.*

__Affirmation__– Father, I thank you for grace, your unmerited, undeserved favor, provided for me because of Christ death on the cross. Thank you that I can experience it more and more each day, in Jesus' name. Amen!

YOU ARE A SON OF GOD

- **_John 1:12 –_** _All who receive him, to those who believe in his name, he gave the right to become children of God._

- **_John 1:17_** _- You are not under the law of Moses; you are under Grace and truth of Jesus Christ. This means you are not a slave or servant, you are a SON!!! Read -_ **_Hebrews 3:5-6_**

- **_Romans 8:15 NLT -_** _So you have not received a spirit that makes you fearful slaves. Instead, you received God's spirit when he adopted you as his own children. Now we call him, "Abba, Father."_

- **_Galatians 3:26 - 29 NLT -_** _For you are all children of God through faith in Christ Jesus. And all who have been united with Christ in bap-_

tism have put on Christ, like putting on new clothes. There is no longer Jew or Gentile, slave or free, male, and female. For you are all one in Christ Jesus, you are the true children of Abraham. You are heirs, and God's promise to Abraham belongs to you.

- ***Galatians 4:4 -7 NLT -*** *But when the right time came, God sent his Son, born of a woman, subject to the law. God sent him to buy freedom for us who were slaves to the law, so he could adopt us as his very own children. And because we are his children, God has sent the Spirit of his Son into our hearts, prompting us to call out "Abba, Father." Now, you are no longer a slave but God's own child. And since you are his child, God has made you, his HEIR.*

- ***1 John 4:13 NLT*** *– And God has given us his Spirit as proof that we live in him and he in us.*

- ***1 John 4:16-19 NLT*** *– We know how much God loves us, and we have put our trust in his love. God is love, and all who live in love, live in God, and God lives in them...as we live in God, our* *love grows more perfect...we will not be afraid on the day of judgment, but we can face him with confidence because we live like Jesus here in this world.*

- ***Ephesians 1:5-6 NLT*** *God decided in advance to adopt us into his own family by bringing us to himself through Christ Jesus. This is what he wanted to do, and it gave him great pleasure. So, we praise God for his glorious grace he has poured out on us who belong to his dear Son.*

<u>*Affirmation*</u>– *Father, I thank you that through receiving Jesus Christ as Lord, I have been made a child of my heavenly Father. Thank you for Christ displaying his love on the cross for me. In Jesus' name, Amen!*

THE BLOOD OF JESUS

- **_Ephesians 1:7 –_** *In HIM we have redemption through his blood, forgiveness of sins according to the riches of God's grace.*

- To sin means to "miss the mark." This verse highlights that the blood of Jesus serves as payment for our sins, restoring our relationship with God. Our lives are now filled with GRACE and MERCY.

- **_Leviticus 16:1-5_** *- In the Old Testament there was the ceremony of Day of Atonement, highest holy day of the Jewish calendar. The high priest of that day made sacrifice for the sins of the people on this day using the blood of bulls and goats as sin offering providing confident forgiveness of sins. The high priest would enter the holy of holies or God's presence and it was only done once a year.*

- ***<u>What did Jesus say about atonement? John 10:17-18 NLT</u>*** – *"The Father loves me because I sacrifice my life so I may take it back again. No man taketh it from me, but I lay it down of myself. I have power to lay it down, and I have power to take it again."*

- Jesus was the only person qualified to be our savior because He is the only person who ever lived on earth who did not sin.

- *We now have been justified through faith and have direct access to God through Christ, by **<u>grace through faith</u>** – **<u>Ephesians 5-2</u>***

- ***<u>1 John 1:7</u>*** – *But if we walk in the light, as he is in the light, we have fellowship with one another, and the blood of Jesus, HIS SON, purifies (or cleanses) us from ALL sin.*

- ***<u>Romans 6:23 -</u>*** *"For the wages of sin is death, but the gift of God is eternal life in Christ Jesus our Lord." (Jesus became our ransom or our compensation paid!)*

- **_Romans 3:22-26-_** *This righteousness is given through faith in Jesus Christ to ALL who believe. There is no difference between Jew and Gentile, for ALL have sinned and fall short of the Glory of God and are justified freely by grace through the redemption that came by Christ Jesus. God presented Christ as a sacrifice of atonement, through the shedding of his blood-to be received by faith. He did this to demonstrate his righteousness, because in his forbearance he had left the sins committed beforehand unpunished-he did it to demonstrate his righteousness at the present time, to be just and the one who justifies those of faith in Jesus.*

- **_1 John 1:8-10 -_** *If we claim to be without sin, we deceive ourselves and the truth is not in us. If we confess our sins, he is faithful and just and will forgive us our sins and purify us from ALL unrighteousness. If we claim we have not sinned, we make him out to be a liar and his word is not in us.*

- **_Access to God's presence. Hebrews 10:19 –_** "We have confidence to enter the holy places by the blood of Jesus."

- ***Hebrews 10:10 -*** *"We have been made sancti-fied (or holy) through the offering of the body of Jesus Christ once for all."*

- ***Ephesians 2:13 -*** *But now in Christ Jesus you who were once far away have been brought near by the blood of Christ.*

- Because we are Christian, we can have confidence as you approach God with your prayers and worship, because you are no longer far away from him. Remember because you have received Jesus "all who have received him have been made children of God (John 1:12)

- ***Revelation 12:11*** *"Conquered by the blood of the lamb and the word of our testimony."*

- ***Hebrews 4:16*** *– Let us approach God's throne of grace with confidence, so that we may receive mercy and find grace to help us in our time of need.*

- **<u>Romans 4:8 –</u>** *Blessed is the one whose sin the Lord will NEVER count against them."*

- **<u>2 Corinthians 5:18-21 NLT –</u>** *"And all of this is a gift from God, who brought us back to himself through Christ. And God has given us this task of reconciling people to him. For God was in Christ, reconciling the world to himself, no longer counting people's sins against them. And he gave us this wonderful message of reconciliation. So, we are Christ's ambassadors; God is making his appeal through us. We speak for Christ when we plead, "Come back to God!" For God made Christ, who never sinned, to be the offering for our sin, so that we could be made right (or the righteousness) with God through Christ."*

<u>Affirmation</u>– Father, I thank you for the shed blood of Jesus that has washed away all my sins, past, present, and future. Thank you, Lord, for loving me so much that you would sacrifice your only son so I could enter a relationship with you In Jesus' name, Amen!

SPEAK THE WORD

- **_Proverbs 6:2 –_** _You have been trapped by what you said, ensnared by the words of your mouth. NLT "Caught by what you said."_

- **_Proverbs 18:21 NLT –_** _The tongue can bring death or life; those who love to talk will reap the consequences._

- **_Hebrews 4:14 -_** _Therefore, since we have a great high priest who has ascended into heaven, Jesus the Son of God, let us hold firmly to the faith we profess. Profess means – To claim, to affirm one's faith. Example: "he had professed his love for her/him"_

- **_Sometimes, what we blame on the devil is not really him at all. We may be experiencing the consequences of our own negative_** _**confessions. Your words will either breathe life into a situation or bring death to it. Your words are a powerful weapon.**_

- _**The tense in which you declare something is crucial. Hebrews 11:1 says -**_ _NOW Faith is the substance of things hoped for, the evidence of things not seen._ (_**Meaning -**_ _is about having confidence and hope in the promised word of God revealed to you. It is taking God at His words knowing that He is too faithful to fail and will never go back on His promises because He is not a man that He should lie... Numbers 23:19)_

- _**Romans 4:17 NLT -**_ _That is what the scriptures mean when God told him, "I have made you the father of many nations." This happened because Abraham believed in the God who brings the dead back to life and who creates new things out of nothing._ _**Another translation**_ _– "calls those things that be not as though they were."_

- ***<u>Romans 10:9-10 NLT</u>*** *If you confess with your mouth that Jesus is Lord and believe in your heart that God raised him from the dead, you will be saved. For it is by believing in your heart that you are made right with God, and it is by confessing with your mouth that you are saved.*

- ***<u>Remember 2 Corinthians 4:13 NLT</u>*** *– "I believe in God, so I spoke." (We have the same spirit of faith as our heavenly Father.)*

Examples of words spoken

- ***Genesis 1:1 – 29 –*** *As God was created the heavens and earth the bible records, he spoke things in existence 10 times.* ***Verse 31 says*** *– God saw all that he had made, and it was very good!*

- ***Genesis 1:26*** *– We are made in the image of God. (Image and Likeness)*

- ***Speaking FEAR is the opposite of speaking FAITH!***

- ***Job 3:25-26 –*** *"What I feared has come upon me; what I dreaded has happened to me. I have no peace, no quietness; I have no rest, but only turmoil."*

- **_Job 22:28 –_** _Thou shalt also decree a thing, and it shall be established. What you decide on will be done, and light will shine on your ways._

- **_Matthew 8:5-13 -_** _The faith of the Roman Centurion_

- **_Matthew 9:20 -_** _Women with the issue of blood for 12 years says to herself" If I only touch his garment, I will be healed._

- **_Mark 11: 12-24 –_** _Jesus curses the fig tree, says "Have Faith in God."_

- **_2 Corinthians 1:20 NIV -_** _For no matter how many promises God has made, they are "YES" in Christ. And so, through him the "AMEN" (so be it) is spoken by us to the glory of God._

Affirmation– Father, I thank you for giving me the authority to speak your word like Christ because of my faith in what Jesus has done. I thank you that as Jesus is, so am I in this world. In Jesus' name, Amen!

SPEAK THE WORD - CONFESSIONS

1. Father, I thank you that faith in the blood of Jesus has placed me in right-standing with you. I thank you that I've received the abundance of grace and the gift of righteousness, so I've already been made righteous! As a result, I have every right to experience God's best in your life. (Romans 5:17 and 2 Corinthians 5:21)

2. *Father, I thank you that because of Jesus, I can declare that I am the righteousness of God. I have been released from the bondage of sin, and I am free to exercise my rights as a born-again believer. I have a right to prosper in every area of my life. (Romans 6:14)*

3. *Father, I thank you that in the name of Jesus, the Word of God is my guarantee that I can speak as God speaks and call into existence ev-*

erything that I need to succeed. I take authority over sickness, disease, poverty, and insufficiency, and I rule as a king in life! (Romans 4:17)

4. *Father, I thank you that in the name of Jesus, I declare that I have a blood-bought right to answered prayer. The Word of God is my guarantee. Father, by prayer, supplication, and with thanksgiving, I can make my requests known to You. You hear the prayer of the righteous and answer them. Your eyes are on me, and your ears are open to hear my prayers. (Philippians 4:6, James 5:16)*

5. *Father, I thank you that I have the mind of Christ, and I remember ALL things! (1 Corinthians 2:16)*

6. *Father, I thank you, I am connected to Christ Jesus, and I am anointed. In everything I do, I am more than a conqueror. Because I abide in You, and Your Word abides in me, I see the manifestation of answered prayer. When I speak Your Word, it does not return without accomplishing what it was sent to do. (Isaiah 55:11, Romans 8:37)*

7. *Father, I thank You that I walk in favor with You and with man. Wherever I go and whatever I do, your favor goes before me. The effectual fervent prayer of a righteous person avails much. Therefore, I believe I will receive what I pray for right now. In Jesus' name, Amen! (Luke 2:52)*

8. Father, I thank you for your favor that surrounds and protects me like a shield (Psalm 5:12).

9. *Father, I thank you that you are pleased with me, and your favor endures for a lifetime (Psalm 30:5, AMP)*

10. Jesus is the Apostle and High Priest over my profession, and what I profess is the Word of God concerning favor over my life (Hebrews 3:1).

11. Like Joseph, I prosper wherever I go, and in every situation. The Lord is always with me. I, too, experienced preferential treatment (Genesis 39:1-6, 21).

12. Because the favor of God shields me, no sickness or disease has a right to live in my body (Deuteronomy 7:15; Psalm 5:12).

13. Because I am God's "favorite," I prosper in every area of my life-spiritually, physically, financially, socially, and mentally (3 John 2).

14. *In the name of Jesus, I declare that my body is the temple of the Holy Ghost, and I glorify God with it. I present a healthy body to God and discipline myself not to overeat. I only eat food that promotes health. The life of God flows through my spirit, soul, and body, and brings healing to every fiber of my being. I am redeemed from the curse of the law, and no weapon of sickness or disease formed against me will prosper. Amen! (1 Corinthians 6:19-20, Romans 12:1, John 4:14, Galatians 3:13, Isaiah 54:17)*

15. *In the name of Jesus, I declare that I am in covenant with God. I have the peace of God; therefore, I am whole in every area. There is nothing missing or broken in my life. I am empowered*

by God to succeed in everything that I do. I am prosperous and equipped to fulfill His perfect will for my life! (Isaiah 54:10, Ezekiel 34:25; 37:26, 3 John 2, Deuteronomy 28:2-8)

16. I am the body of Christ, redeemed from the curse. Because Jesus bore my sicknesses and carried my diseases in His own body, by HIS stripes, I am healed. I forbid sickness and disease from operating in my body. Every organ, every tissue, every bone, and every cell of my body functions in the perfection in which God created it to function. (Isaiah 53:5, 1 Peter 2:24)

SEEK FIRST THE KINGDOM OF GOD

- ***Matthew 6:33 –*** *But seek ye first the kingdom of God, and his righteousness; and all these things will be added to unto you.*
- ***NLT says -*** *Above all else, live righteously, and he will give you everything you need!*
- ***Luke 17:21 NLT -*** *Jesus says, "The Kingdom of God is within you."*

"So above all, constantly seek God's kingdom and his righteousness, then all these less important things will be given to you abundantly. Refuse to worry about tomorrow, but deal with each challenge that comes your way, one day at a time. Tomorrow will take care of itself."

- ***Matthew 6:25 -27 NLT –*** *That is why I tell you not to worry about everyday life, whether you have enough food and drink, or enough clothes to wear. Look at the birds. They don't plant or* *harvest or store food in barns, for your heavenly Father feeds them. Aren't you more valuable to him than they are? Can all your worries add a single moment to your life?*

- **_Matthew 6:28- 30 NLT -_** *Talks about why worry about clothing. Compares lilies in the field to Solomon's clothes, saying "in all Solomon's glory he wasn't dressed as well as they are.*

- **_Matthew 6:31,32 NLT –_** *"So don't worry about these things, saying, what will be eat, drink, or wear? These things dominate the thoughts of unbelievers, but your heavenly Father already knows **_ALL YOUR NEEDS!!_***

- **_1 Peter 5:5,6 and 7 -_** *God opposes or resists the proud but favors the humble. So, humble yourselves under the mighty hand of God, and at the right time he will lift you up in honor. Give ALL YOUR WORRIES AND CARES TO GOD, FOR HE CARES ABOUT YOU.*

Affirmation– Father, I thank you that I can seek you first, knowing that you have made provision for all my needs. In Jesus' name, Amen!

FOCUS ON OTHERS

- **_Matthew 25:35 NLT_** – *For I was hungry, and you fed me, I was thirsty, and you gave me a drink, I was a stranger, and you invited me into your home. I was naked, and you gave me clothing. I was sick and you cared for me. I was in prison, and you visited me. "Then these righteous ones will reply, Lord, when did we ever see you hungry, and feed you? Or thirsty and give you something to drink? Or a stranger and show you hospitality? Or naked and give you clothing? When did we ever see you sick or in prison and visit you? And the King will say, I tell you the truth, when you did it to one of the least of these my brothers and sisters, you were doing it to ME!*

- **_Romans 12:9,10,11,12 and 13_** – *Don't just pretend to love others. Really love them. Hate what is wrong. Hold tightly to what is good. Love each other with genuine affection and take in honoring each other. Never be lazy but* *work hard and serve the Lord enthusiastically. Rejoice in our confident hope. Be patient in trouble and keep on praying. When God's people are in need, be ready to help them. Always be eager to practice hospitality.*

<u>*Affirmation*</u>*– Father, I thank you for giving me the ability to serve others. I thank you for blessing me to be a blessing to others. Thank you for giving me compassion for people and the strength to use my gifts and talents to help them. In Jesus' name, Amen!*

RESTING IN CHRIST

- ***Matthew 11:28-30 – NLT*** – *Jesus says "Come to me, all of you who are weary and carry heavy, and I will give you rest. Take my yoke upon you. Let me teach you, because I am humble and gentle at heart, and you will find rest for your souls. For my yoke is easy to bear, and the burden I give you is light.*

- ***Hebrews 4: -*** *Read about the promised rest for God's people.* ***4:11 NLT*** *So let us do our best to enter that rest. Another word is* ***peace.***

1 Peter 5:6-7 *-Humble yourselves, under God's mighty hand, that he may lift you up in due time. Cast all your anxiety on him because he cares for you.*

Affirmation– *Father, I thank you for giving me the ability to rest in you. Thank you for taking my worry, fear, and anxiety, and in exchange, giving me your peace and calm in all situations of my life. in Jesus' name, Amen*

RIGHTEOUS AND JUSTIFIED BY FAITH

- **_Matthew 6:33 –_** _But seek ye first the kingdom of God, and his righteousness; and all these things will be added to unto you._

- **_Romans 14:17 -_** _For the kingdom of God is not a matter food or drink, but righteousness, and peace, and joy in the Holy Spirit._

- **_Galatians 3:23 NLT -_** _Before the way of faith in Christ was available to us, we were placed under guard by the law. We were kept in protective custody, so to speak, until the way of faith was revealed._

- **_Galatians 3:24 and 25 NLT -_** _Let me put it another way. The law was our guardian until Christ came; it protected us until we could be made right with God through faith. And now_ *that the way of faith has come, we no longer need the law as our guardian.*

- **_Galatians 3:26 and 27 NLT -_** *For you are all children of God through faith in Christ Jesus. And all who have been united with Christ in baptism have put on Christ, like putting on new clothes.*

- **_Galatians 3:28 NLT -_** *There is no longer Jew or Gentile, slave or free, male, or female. For you are all one in Christ Jesus. And now that you belong to Christ, you are true children of Abraham. You are his heirs, and God's promise to Abraham belongs to you.*

- **_Romans 4:13 NLT -_** *Clearly, God's promise to give the whole earth (**be an heir of the world**) to Abraham and his descendants was based not on his obedience to God's law, but on a right relationship with God that comes by faith. **Romans 8:16-17 –** heirs of God and joint heirs with Christ.*

- ***Greek word for World*** – Kosmos – meaning "the whole circle of earthly goods, endowments, riches, advantages, and pleasures. This is the promise God made to Abraham (Genesis 12:2).

- ***Romans 4:14 NLT*** – *If God's promise is only for those who obey the law, then faith is not necessary, and the promise is pointless. For the law always brings punishment on those who try to obey it. (The only way to avoid breaking the law is to have no law to break!)*

- ***Romans 4:16 NLT*** – *So the promise is received by faith. It is given as a FREE gift. And we are all certain to receive it, whether or not we live according to the law of Moses if we have faith like Abraham's. For Abraham is the father of all who BELIEVE.*

- ***Psalms 84:11 ESV*** - *For the Lord God is a sun and a shield; the Lord gives grace and glory (favor and honor). No good thing does he withhold from those who walk uprightly. (Another translation is "from those whose walk is blameless.") How to do this? Follow Christ!*

Affirmation– _Father, I thank you that faith in Jesus has put me in right standing with you. Thank you that I am justified by faith and have received the inheritance that has come by way of faith in Christ. In Jesus' name, Amen!_

⌐ JOY IN SUFFERING ⌐

- ***James 1:2:3 and 4 NLT –*** *Dear brothers and sisters, when troubles come your way, consider it an opportunity for great joy. (another translation "Count it all joy"). For you know that when your faith is tested, your endurance has a chance to grow. So let it grow, for when your endurance is fully developed, you will be perfect and complete, needing nothing.*

- ***James 1:5 NLT -*** *If you need wisdom, ask our generous God, and he will give it to you. He will NOT rebuke you for asking.*

- ***James 1:6, 7 and 8 NLT -*** *But when you ask him, be sure that your faith is in God alone. Do not waver, for a person with divided loyalty is as unsettled as a wave of the sea that is blown and tossed by the wind. Such people should not expect to receive anything from the Lord. Their* *loyalty is divided between God and the world, and they are unstable in everything they do.*

- **_Romans 8:28 NLT -_** *And we know that God causes everything to work together for the good of those who love God and are called according to his purpose for them.*

- **_1 Thessalonians 5:16 NLT –_** *Always be joyful.*

- **_1 Thessalonians 5:17 NLT –_** *Never stop praying.*

- **_1 Thessalonians 5:18 NLT -_** *Be thankful in all circumstances, for this is God's will for you who belong to Christ Jesus.*

Affirmation– Father, I thank you for leading me through all circumstances. I trust that you will never leave me or forsake me. I thank you for these trials as they will make me stronger, wiser, and closer to you. In Jesus' name, Amen!

THE FAVOR OF GOD Part 2

Ephesians 2:8 – For it is by grace (**_favor_**) you have been saved, through faith-and this is not from yourself, it is the gift of God. AMP version says [God's remarkable compassion and favor drawing you to Christ].

What is the main message of Galatians chapter 1?

A group of Christians preaching a gospel of legalism (depending on the law or salvation), rather than grace. Paul's main purpose in writing the letter to the Galatians was to reiterate the true nature of the gospel: we are justified (made righteous) and sanctified (made more Christlike) **_through our faith in Jesus Christ alone_**.

Grace is the basis for the Christian faith. How do you receive God's grace? **_By Trusting Jesus Christ_**.

Examples of the Favor of God

- God granting good will or kindness to us – Psalms 37-4

- God bestowing his love on you as a token of his regard for you – Romans 5:8, John 14:14, Psalms 34:15.

- Favor of God represents preferential treatment – This is his way of helping us!

- Represents advantages – things working out in your favor even if no one else knows about it.

Favor is to show God is your source, he is the ONLY source you need!

Favor means to endorse. God has endorsed you!

Favor means support. God has supported you!

Favor means to assist. God has assisted you!

Favor makes things easier. Sweatless victories

Affirmation– Father, I thank you for giving me your divine favor. Jesus walked in wisdom, stature, and favor with you and man, I believe I do the same in every area of my life. In Jesus' name, Amen!

GRACE AND FAITH

How important is the Grace of God? There are 131 uses of the word grace in the ESV — 124 in the New Testament, 86 of which are from the apostle Paul, which means two-thirds of all the uses of the word grace in the Bible are in one author: Paul.

Ephesians 2:8 – For it is by grace (**_favor_**) you have been saved, through faith-and this is not from yourself, it is the gift of God. AMP version says [God's remarkable compassion and favor drawing you to Christ].

- **_Grace not only offers salvation but secures it._**

Romans 5:20-21 NLT – God's law was given so that all people could see how sinful they were. But as people sinned more and more, God's wonderful grace became more abundant. So just as sin ruled over all people and brought them to death, now God's wonderful grace rules instead, giving is right standing with God and resulting in eternal life through Jesus Christ our Lord.

- **_The law is the strength of sin (1 Corinthians 15:56_** – *this means the law of Moses, at that time, wasn't the cure for sin but instead gave strength or life to people's sins because no one could keep the laws. Only Jesus Christ could fulfill the law because though he was tempted, he never sinned.*

2 Corinthians 12:9-10 - *But he said to me, my grace is sufficient for you, for my power is made perfect in weakness." Therefore, I will boast all the more gladly of my weaknesses, so that the power of Christ may rest upon me. For the sake of Christ, then, I am content with weaknesses, insults, hardships, persecutions, and calamities. For when I am weak, then I am strong.*

- **_Grace is the strength of salvation; it comes from God's love for us (Roman 8:31-39)_**

  Hebrews 4:15-16 - *For we do not have a high priest who is unable to sympathize with our weaknesses, but one who in every respect has been tempted as we are, yet without sin. Let us then with confidence draw near to the throne of grace, that we may receive mercy and find grace to help in time of need.*

- **_Jesus was able to identify with us because of his human experience and sufferings._**

  John 1:16-17 - *For from his fullness we have all received grace upon grace. For the law was given through Moses; grace and truth came through Jesus Christ.*

- **_Grace shows God's (unmerited) favor that brings blessing and joy._**

  James 4:6 - *But he gives more grace. Therefore, it says, "God opposes the proud but gives grace to the humble."*

- ***Opposes means resists the proud.***

  Romans 6:14 - *For sin will have no dominion over you, since you are not under law but under grace.*

- ***You are no longer controlled by a law that was for Jews, you live under the new covenant in Christ (Romans 3:24;4:16;5:2, 15-21)***

  Titus 2:11-14 - *For the grace of God has appeared that offers salvation to all people. It teaches us to say "No" to ungodliness and worldly passions, and to live self-controlled, upright, and godly lives in the present age, while we wait for the blessed hope, the appearing of the glory of our great God and Savior, Jesus Christ, who gave himself for us to redeem us from all wickedness and to purify for himself a people that are his very own, eager to do what is good.*

- **_Grace teaches us to say NO to sin and YES to godly living through faith in Christ._**

  Make this confession daily. The Lord is with ME (insert your name here), and I'm a successful person. I have the Favor of God!

Affirmation– Father, I thank you that I'm not under the old laws of Moses. When I fall short, I'm not condemned, because Christ fulfilled the law on my behalf. I now live under Your grace. I thank you for bringing me into this new covenant. In Jesus' name, Amen!

THE FINISHED WORK OF CHRIST/
WHAT GRACE HAS MADE AVAILABLE

__The finished work of Christ refers__ primarily to His sacrificial death on the cross. __That's where the judgment of God against our sins was endured by Christ. John 19:30, 2 Corinthians 5:21.__

- *I know God loves me. He's given us the holy spirit to fill our hearts with His love. Faith works by love. __Romans 5:5 Galatians 5:6__*

- *Believe – Evidence of believing is "resting" in the finished works of Jesus Christ. __Hebrews 4__*

- *Ways of resting: Prayer, putting on favorite praise and worship songs. When you're resting in Jesus, he is working for you. When you're trying to do all the work he rests. Trust and depend on Him! He said he will never leave or forsake us.* **Hebrews 13:5**

- *"**When you're resting in Him, you'll hear from him. Listen and obey." (SURRENDER)***

- *Speaking. Let the redeemed of the Lord "Say so." – we believe therefore we speak. Behold I gave you power. Release your authority.* **Psalms 107:2. 2 Corinthians 4:13. Luke 10:19**

- *Acknowledge what grace has provided every good thing in you which is by Christ Jesus. You're blessed with all spiritual blessings, in heavenly places in Christ.* **Philemon 4:6. Ephesians 1:3.**

- *Give thanks!!* **1 Thessalonians 5: 16, 17, 18.**

- *Be content regardless of the circumstances.* **Philippians 4:11**

- *Focus on helping others. Be a giver.* **Luke 6:38**

Acknowledge being crucified with Christ

- ***Galatians 2:20*** – *"I have been crucified with Christ and I no longer live, but Christ lives in me. The life I now live in the body, I live by faith in the Son of God., who loved me and gave himself for me." (Other translation says, "**Faith of the Son of God**.")*

- ***Galatians 2:21 -*** *"I do not frustrate (set aside, treat as meaningless) for if righteousness comes through the law, then Christ died in vain (for nothing).*

Affirmation– Father, I thank you for Christ's' finished work on the cross for my sake. I thank you that I can rest my life in him because of how much he loves me in Jesus' name. Amen!

Come BOLDLY to the throne of Grace

- **_Hebrews 4:14, 15 NLT -_** *Therefore, since we have a great high priest who has entered heaven, Jesus the Son of God, let us hold firmly to faith we believe (another translation is profess. Profess means – To claim, to affirm one's faith in. Example: "he had professed his love for her/him"). This High Priest of ours understands our weaknesses, for he faced all the same testing we do, yet he did not sin.*

- **_Hebrews 4:16 NLT -_** *So let us come **BOLDY** to the throne of our gracious of God. There we will receive his mercy, and we will find grace to help us when we need it most.*

- **_Romans 4:13 NLT –_** *Clearly, God's promise to give the whole earth to Abraham (another translation – heir of the world) and his descendants (offspring) was based not on obedience* *to God's law, but on a right relationship with God that comes by faith.*

- Expect God to help you, he has provided us access to him through Jesus (Romans 5:2)

- Remember you have the ABUNDANCE OF GRACE and THE GIFT OF RIGHTEOUSNESS

- **<u>Romans 5:17 -</u>** *For the sin of one man, Adam, caused death to rule over many. But even greater is God's wonderful GRACE (or another translation - abundance of Grace) and his gift of righteousness, for all who receive it will live triumph over sin and death through this one man, JESUS CHRIST!*

- When you confess you are the righteousness of God in Christ, you bring glory to God

<u>*Affirmation*</u>*– Father, I thank you that I can come boldly to you and without fear. I thank you for providing me with abundant grace and the gift of righteousness. In Jesus' name, Amen!*

⌐ The Gift of Righteousness ¬

- **_Romans 5:17 -_** _For the sin of one man, Adam, caused death to rule over many. But even greater is God's wonderful GRACE (or another translation - abundance of Grace) and his gift of righteousness, for all who receive it will live triumph over sin and death through this one man, JESUS CHRIST!_

- _This is a **GIFT**, not a reward or an award. Grace comes through Jesus_

- _To try and justify yourself through your works is an **Abomination**. God hates or finds offensive._

- _**Proverbs 17:15**. Acquitting the guilty and condemning the innocent - The Lord detests them both. Why? Because it's PRIDE._

- ***When God sees you in Christ, He sees:***
  - the blood of Jesus
  - Complete forgiveness
  - Blessing and favor
  - Perfect RIGHETOUSNESS (in right standing with him)

- ***1 John 4:17 – As Jesus is, so are we in this world.***

- ***When you confess you are the righteousness of God in Christ, you bring glory to God***

- ***Matthew 6:33 –*** *says "HIS" righteousness.* ***God never sees Jesus without seeing me in him and him in me. He doesn't see you outside of Jesus! Jesus is the measure of our righteousness.***

- *How righteous are you? As righteous as Jesus who is the measure of our righteous-ness.*

Affirmation– Father, I thank You that when You look at me, You see me in Christ. You see Your Son—righteous, accepted, and dearly loved. I receive this gift of righteousness by faith and confess it boldly. Thank You for loving me, saving me, and calling me Your own. In Jesus' name, Amen!

The Gift of Righteousness Part 2

- *__Matthew 6:33 –__ says "HIS" righteousness. **God never sees Jesus without seeing me in him and him in me. He doesn't see you outside of Jesus! Jesus is the measure of our righteousness.***

- *Seeking God's kingdom and is not going to the mission field or on the streets*

- *__Romans 14:17__ For the kingdom of God is not a matter of eating and drinking, but righteousness, peace, and joy in the Holy Spirit.*

- Let go of worry, seek his righteousness, and all things will be added to you as an inheritance in Christ.

- Everything in your life is tied to HIS RIGH-TEOUSNESS...if you are in Christ.

- Live free from stress – 1 Peter 5:6,7

- Have power over sin – Romans 6:14

- Blessings can flow to you and through you – 2 Corinthians 9:8

- *Shows our dependence on God/Abba Father/ Daddy through* **_Christ._**

- **_Luke 18:10-14_** *Jesus tells a story – "Two men went up to the temple to pray, one a Pharisee and the other a tax collector. The Pharisee stood by himself and prayed; God, I thank you that I am not like other people-robbers, evildo-ers, adulterers-or even like this tax collector. I fast a week and give a tenth of all I get. But the tax collector stood at a distance, He would not even look up to heaven, but beat his breast and said, God have mercy on me, a sinner." I tell* *you that this man, rather than the other, went home __justified (or righteous)__ before God. For all those who exalt themselves will be humbled, and those who humble themselves will be exalted.*

- *How to please God – exercise your faith in HIS righteousness. Since "faith pleases him, and he is a rewarder of those who diligently seek him."* __Hebrews 11:6__

Affirmation– *Father, I thank you for what Christ has done at the cross for me. I can confess that I am indeed the righteousness of God. Thank you for providing me with this benefit as a child of God. In Jesus' name, Amen!*

How do you frustrate the Grace of God?

- *Not receiving his Grace*

- *Trying to earn something that his Grace has already made available to us (Works)*

- *You're going to need the Grace or Unmerited Favor to fulfill the assignment God has given you. This is for your life.*

Reminder about the Favor of God

- ***2 Corinthians 9:8 -*** And God is able to make all grace (every ***favor*** and earthly blessing) come to you in abundance so that you may always and under all circumstances and whatever the need be self-sufficient {possessing enough to require no aid or support and furnished in abundance for every good and charitable donation}.

- ***Psalms 5:12 -*** Surely, Lord, you bless the righteous; you surround them with your ***favor*** as with a shield."

- ***Psalms 23:6*** – Surely Goodness (***favor***) and mercy shall follow me all the days of my life.

- ***Psalms 84:11*** – The Lord gives ***favor*** and honor, no good thing will he withhold from the righteous.

- _**Luke 2:52**_ – Jesus grew in wisdom, stature, and in _**favor**_ with God and man.

Affirmation– _Father, I thank you that I have the Favor of God. I thank you for that I can apply it to every situation in my life. In Jesus' name, Amen!_

⌐ REJOICE ⌐

**No matter what season of life you're in, God calls you to live with joy, prayer, and gratitude. These three responses aren't just good habits; they are God's will for His children.**

- _**1 Thessalonians 5:16 NLT –** Always be joyful._

- _**1 Thessalonians 5:17 NLT –** Never stop praying._

- _**1 Thessalonians 5:18 NLT -** Be thankful in all circumstances, for this is God's will for you who belong to Christ Jesus._

- _**Romans 8:28 NLT -** And we know that God causes everything to work together for the good of those who love God and are called according to his purpose for them._

Affirmation– *Father, I want to take a moment and thank you not because of what you can do or have done for me, but just because of who YOU are. I thank you so much in Jesus' name. Amen!*

Right with God

- **_Romans 3:22 NLT_** _"We are made right with God by placing our faith in Jesus Christ. And this is true for everyone who believes, no matter who we are. "_

- **_1 Corinthians 1:30 NLT_** – _Christ made us right with God; he made us pure and holy, and freed us from sin._

- _Being made right with God can only be **RECEIVED**, not achieved._

- **_1 Corinthians 1:31 NLT_** – _Therefore, as the Scriptures say, "If you want to boast, boast only about the Lord." Referencing **Romans 4:2** – If Abraham were justified by works, he could boast- but not before God._

- **_Ephesians 2:8 NLT_** – God saved you by his grace when you believed. And you can't take credit for this; it's a gift from God.

- **_Ephesians 2:9 NLT_** – Salvation is not a reward for the good things we have done, so none of us can boast about it.

- **_Ephesians 2:10 NLT_** – FOR WE ARE GOD's MASTERPIECE (other translations say – "workmanship". He has created us anew in Jesus Christ, so we can do the good things he planned for us long ago.

- **_Philippians 2:13 NLT-_** For God is working in you, giving you the desire and power to do what pleases him.

Affirmation– Father, I thank you that my faith in Christ is what has brought me into a right relationship with you. Thank you for being my God, my father, my Lord, and Savior. In Jesus' name, Amen!

God has dealt to us the measure of FAITH

- **_Romans 3:22 NLT –_** says, "We are made right with God by placing our faith in Jesus Christ. And this is true for everyone who believes, no matter who we are. "

- **_Galatians 5:6 NLT_** - For when we place our faith in Christ Jesus, there is no benefit in being circumcised or being uncircumcised. What is important is FAITH expressing itself in **_LOVE_**. (Other translations say, "working through love or by love.")

- **_LOVE_** is an action word – expressing through your actions.

- **_Romans 12:3 NLT_** – Because of this privilege and authority God has given me, I give each of you this warning; Don't think you are better *than you really are. Be honest in your evalua-tion of yourselves, measuring yourselves by the faith God has given us. (Sounds like a **GIFT**)*

- ***Philippians 2:13 NLT-*** *For God is working in you, giving you the desire and power to do what pleases him.*

- *What is working for you? LOVE, FAITH, RIGH-TEOUSNESS, JOY, PEACE all by the Holy Spirt (**Romans 14:17 and 1 John 4:12-13**)*

- *Remember FAITH pleases him **(Hebrews 11:6)***

- ***Galatians 2:20 NLT*** *– My old self has been cru-cified with Christ. It is no longer I who live, but Christ lives in me. So, I live in this earthly body by trusting in the Son of God, who loved me and gave himself for me. (Another translation: **Faith in or of the Son of God!**)*

- We are to live our lives resting in the faith of the son of God – JESUS, and this can only be done by taking the following steps:

- You don't have to wonder if your faith is enough.

- *You don't have to strive to build it alone.*

- *You've been given His faith, and that's more than enough.*

- *The Spirit of Christ now lives in you. (__Romans 5:5 and Galatians 4:6-7__)*

<u>Affirmation</u>– *Father, I thank you for giving me the faith of Christ. The same faith that raised him from the dead now lives and works in me. I thank you in Jesus' name. Amen!*

Prayer

- **_Matthew 6:5 NLT–_** _When you pray, don't be like hypocrites who love to pray publicly on street corners and in synagogues where everyone can see them. I tell you the truth, that is all the reward they will ever get._

- **_Matthew 6:6 NLT_** _- But when you pray, go away by yourself, shut the door behind you, and pray to the Father in private._Then your father, who sees everything, will reward you._

- **_Matthew 6:7-8 NLT_ –** _When you pray, don't babble on and on as people of other religions do. They think their prayers are answered merely by repeating their words again and again. Don't be like them, for your father knows exactly what you need even before you ask him!_

- Jesus teaches that prayer should be a private time between our Father (God) and the worshipper. That does not mean it is wrong to pray with others; it means that prayers should be sincere and for the right motives.

- *Jesus emphasized humility, forgiveness, and generous care for our neighbors. Example:* **LOVE**

- **Philippians 4:6-7 NLT -** *Don't worry about anything; instead, pray about everything. Tell God what you need and THANK HIM for all he's done. Then you will experience God's peace, which exceeds anything we can understand. His peace will guard your hearts and minds as you live in Christ Jesus.*

- **John 15:7 – NLT -** *But if you remain in me and my words remain in you, you may ask for anything you want, and it will be granted!*

- **Ephesians 3:20 NLT-** *Now all glory to God, who is able, through his mighty power at work* *within us, to accomplish infinitely more than we might ask or think. (other translations – exceedingly or abundantly and above, more than we can ever ask or think).*

<u>Affirmation</u>– Father, I thank you for giving me the ability to pray. I thank you for my relationship with you and the time I can spend with you, along with the benefit it adds to my life, in Jesus' name. Amen!

Never Stop Praying

- *"Rejoice always; **pray without ceasing**; in everything give thanks; for this is God's will for you in Christ Jesus." – **1 Thessalonians 5:16-18***

- *Jesus tells his disciples through a story that they should always pray and never give up (another translation says, "not faint.")*

- Questions to ask yourself:

- Have you ever experienced a time when you felt you couldn't pray?

- How did it make you feel? How did you handle it?

- Have you ever experienced a time when you were glad that you prayed without ceasing?

- Enter his gates with Thanksgiving. Enter his courts with praise. Bless his name. Psalms 100:4

- *He is a prayer answering God.* **Luke 11:9 and Mark 11:24**

- *He's a covenant keeping God.* **2 Timothy 2:13 and Hebrews 13:5**

- *It's important to know you are LOVED by our heavenly father._* **Romans 8:37-39, Romans 5:8 and 1 John 4:10**

- *It's important to believe you are righteous. A lot of people are so prone to guilt, condemnation.* **2 Corinthians 5:21**

- *Some people have a begging spirit and not a sonship spirit.* **Galatians 3:26 and 1 John 3:1-2**

- *Believers aren't receiving because they aren't believing. You show your believing by speaking* **2 Corinthians 4:13** *How are you speaking? Things don't just happen in your thoughts; they happen by speaking!*

Affirmation– Father, I thank you that I can bring myself to you, not having to hide who I am or what I've done. I thank you, my prayer time with you is powerful and can produce positive, life-changing results in my life in Jesus' name. Amen!

Be ready in season and out

- **_2 Timothy 4:2_** – *Preach the word of God; be prepared in season and out of season, (NLT says, "whether the time is favorable or not.") Patiently correct, rebuke, and encourage your people with good teaching.*

- *Paul told this to Timothy, meaning you must always be ready, always, even if it's an unexpected or inconvenient time for you.*

- **_2 Timothy 2:15_** – *Study to shew thyself approved unto God, a workman that needed not to be ashamed, rightly dividing the word of truth."*

- *This verse is Paul warning Timothy about False Teachers.*

- The word of God has the power to transform life, and we should discipline ourselves to read and study the word (daily, weekly, etc.)

Affirmation– *Father, thank You for calling me to be prepared in every season. Help me to stay grounded in Your Word so I can speak truth with wisdom, recognize deception, and live a life that honors You. Thank You for good teachers and thank You for the Holy Spirit who helps me understand and apply Your truth. In Jesus' name, Amen!*

We love because he first loved us

- **_1 John 4:19 –_** _We love because he first loved us._

- **_Summary_** _– God loves us not because of what we do, but because of who you are. You will never need to earn God's love._

- **_John 17:20-23 NLT–_** _Christ says "I am praying not only for these disciples but also for all who will ever believe in me through their message. I pray that they will all be one, just as you and I are one---as you are in me, Father, and I am in you. And may they be in us so that the world will believe you sent me. I have given them the glory you gave me, so they may be one as we are one. I am in them, and you are in me. May they experience such perfect unity that the world will know that you sent me, and that you love them as much as you love me."_

- Say this to yourself. <u>"God loves me, just as much as he loves his son Jesus!"</u>

RELATED SCRIPTURES ON LOVE

- *John 13:34 - __John 13:34-35 NLT__ – So now I'm giving you a new commandment; Love each other. Just as I have loved you, you should love each other. Your love for one another will prove to the world that you are my disciples.*

- Galatians 5:6 – Faith Works by LOVE.

- 1 Corinthians 13:13 – Faith, Hope and Love but the greatest is LOVE

- If you have God's love, don't you think you have his FAVOR? Don't you think you have his RIGHTEOUSNESS? Romans 5:17 – Abundance of Grace and Gift of Righteousness!

Affirmation– Father, I thank you for loving me even before I came into this covenant of grace with you. I thank you for loving me just like you love Christ. In Jesus' name, Amen!

Abounding Grace

- **_2 Corinthians 9:8_** – _"And God is able to make all grace abound to you, so that having all sufficiency in all things at all times, you may abound in every good work."_

- **_God's ability_** – _Reminds us that God can do ALL things that concern us through his grace._

- **_Generous giving_** – _Encourages us to be generous with the things of God, which will lead to a quality harvest._

- **_Cheerful giving_** - _God loves a cheerful and generous giver, and we should give to give, not to get._

- ***Replenishment*** – *God can replenish whatever we give, so we can be generous on all occasions.*

- ***Summary meaning*** – *God increases the ability of believers who give generously to give even more.*

Affirmation – *Father, I thank You for Your abounding grace in my life. Help me never to hesitate in sharing the blessings You've given me. Teach me to give with joy and to live generously, just as Christ did—the greatest giver of all. In Jesus' name, Amen.*

More and More Grace

- In Christianity, grace is a gift that takes the form of love, divine favor, and a share in God's divine life. It is also seen as God's empowerment that gives people the ability to go beyond their natural abilities.

- In the Bible, God describes himself as gracious (Isaiah 30:18). Grace is a part of God's character (Psalms 103:8). Some ways to grow in grace include Putting Jesus first (Matthew 6:33), coming boldly to the throne of grace (Hebrews 4:16), and turning away from sins (Romans 6:14) and seeking God's forgiveness (Ephesians 1:7).

- 2 Peter 1:2-4 KJV – "Grace and Peace be multiplied to you through the knowledge of God and of Jesus our Lord. NIV says – May God give you more and more grace and peace <u>as you grow in your knowledge of God</u> and Jesus our Lord."

- This is God's promise to his people.

- This is not just knowing facts about God but getting to know <u>HIM</u>!

- Summary – I'm dependent on God the Father through Jesus Christ, my Lord!

- How important is it to spread the message of God's grace?

- Paul says in Galatians 1-8, "Let God's curse fall on anyone, including an angel from heaven, who preaches a different kind of gospel or good news than the one he preached, which is the gospel of God's grace.

<u>Affirmation</u>– Father, I thank you for the message of your grace, which leads to salvation for all who believe. I pray for you to educate and equip me to spread your love through this message. In Jesus' name, Amen.

Let us do good to all people

- Galatians 6:10 ESV – "So then, as we have opportunity, let us do good to everyone, and especially to those who are of the household of faith".

- Galatians 6: 1-10 – Paul talks about we harvest what we plant. The seeds we sow into others will come back to us to reap a harvest of blessing if we don't give up.

Some interpretations of this include

- Broad command - This command applies to everyone, regardless of age, gender, personality, finances, or station in life. (Galatians 3:26-29)

- Use your gifts - This verse encourages people to use their gifts and skills to do good. (1 Peter 4:10)

- Response to God - This verse suggests that people should respond to God and let God's Spirit (holy spirit) do the work of growth in them. (Galatians 5:16-26)

Affirmation– *Father, I thank you for giving me the ability to do good for all people you place in my path. I thank you; I will sow seeds of good and not of evil and be compassionate to those in need, in Jesus' name. Amen!*

Jesus our Savior

Matthew 1:21 – Jesus saved us from our sins.

Galatians 4:4,5 – He redeemed us from the law so we could be made the adoption of sons. Law was made for Jewish people (subject to the law of Moses). Jesus was born as a Jewish man, and he had to be submitted to the law. Religion told Americans and everyone else the law was for you. It was NOT!

Romans 9:4 – God gave the people of Israel his law.

Romans 3:19 – Law was given to Jewish people.

*Matthew 5:17 – Jesus came to **fulfill** the law, not destroy it.*

Romans 10:4 – Christ is the end of the law for everyone who believes.

Hebrews 8:6 – Mediator of a better covenant which was established with better promises.

John 1:17 – Grace and Truth came by Jesus (Law was given by Moses)

1 John 2:2 – His is propitiation for our sins, ransom,

sin offering, peace offering paid for our sins (Jesus paid it ALL for the whole world, every human on the planet.

John 3:16, 17 – God so loved the world, and didn't send his son to condemn the world.

Romans 8:1 – No more condemnation!

<u>Affirmation</u>– Father, I thank you that you sent your son into the world to save us. I thank you, he didn't come to bring condemnation, but that through him we could be born into the family of God. I thank you for this in Jesus' name. Amen!

Joint Heirs with Jesus Christ

- Romans 8:15 ESV – "The Spirit you received does not make you slaves, so that you live in fear again; rather, the Spirit you received brought about your sonship, and by him we cry, Abba, FATHER."

- Romans 8:16 ESV – "The Spirit himself testifies with our spirit that WE ARE GOD'S CHILDREN."

- Romans 8:17 ESV – "If we are children, we are heirs- heirs of God, and joint heirs (or co-heirs) with Christ. (Related scripture- Romans 4:13, you're an heir of the world – Seed of Abraham)

- What does it mean to be a joint heir with Christ?

- Answer – When you accepted Jesus as your Savior and Lord, you joined God's family. You became one of his children, and you received the same rights and privileges that Jesus has!

- Believing and Speaking – Romans 10-10

- 2 Corinthians 4:13 – We having the same spirit of faith, according as it is written, I believed, and therefore have spoken; we also believe, and therefore we speak.

- A spirit of faith boldly declares what it believes and then acts on what it confesses. Read Hebrews 4:11, which talks about RESTING.

- 1 Corinthians 12:3 – It is the Holy Spirit who gives people faith to recognize that "Jesus is Lord."

Affirmation– *Father, I thank you that because of what Christ has done, I'm an heir of God. I thank you for placing your spirit in my heart, making me a joint heir with Christ. I thank you for this in Jesus' name. Amen!*

Better Covenant, Better Promises

- *Hebrews 8 in the Bible explains why Jesus's new covenant is better than the old covenant. It emphasizes that Jesus is the high priest for all believers who serves in a greater place than any earthly temple. The chapter also promises a deeper relationship with God with transformative power.*

- *Jesus's role as priest is superior to the Old Testament system*

- *The old covenant was flawed because it relied on sinful humans*

- *The new covenant is based on better promises*

- *The new covenant offers a more intimate knowledge of God*

The main message of the book of Hebrews is to encourage Christians to remain in faith to Jesus Christ and not return to the Old Covenants of the Law. The book emphasizes that Jesus is superior to all others because he's the only one who died for our sins and that he is worthy of our faith and trust in Him.

Affirmation– Father, I thank you that as a believer in Christ I'm part of the covenant Jesus died for me to inherit. I'm thankful your promises for me are Yes and Amen, in Jesus' name. Amen!

Being in Christ

- **_Romans 3:22 NLT –_** _says, "We are made right with God by placing our faith in Jesus Christ. And this is true for everyone who believes, no matter who we are. "_

- _Colossians 2:9-10 NLT – "For in Christ lives all the fullness of God in human body. So, you also are complete through your union **with Christ**, who is the head over every ruler and authority."_

- Other translations say the word "Deity," which literally means "the state of being God."

- This verse emphasizes the divine nature of Christ, expressing the belief that Jesus embodies the fullness of God in human form or flesh (1 Timothy 3:16)

- Fullness – means he didn't come empty-handed. He brought gifts! i.e., Access to him (Romans 5:2), Abundance of Grace, and the gift of righteousness. (Romans 5:17)

Affirmation– *Father, I thank you for loving me and bringing me into complete union with you through the love and faith of Jesus Christ. I thank you for giving me this benefit. In Jesus' name, Amen!*

I AM CONFESSIONS

- John 14:6 – Jesus declares "I am the way, the truth and the life."

- What are you saying? What's your "I am"

- Joel 3:10 "Let the weak say, I am strong"

- Romans 4:16 Because we're Abraham's offspring by faith we can call into being what does not yet exist. "

- I AM LOVED

- I AM ACCEPTED IN THE BELOVED

- I AM FREE

- I AM A CHILD OF GOD

- I AM A FRIEND OF GOD

- I AM THANKFUL

- I AM GRATEFUL

- I AM REDEEMED

- I AM UNDER THE GRACE OF GOD

- I AM THE RIGHTEOUSNESS OF GOD

- I AM FORGIVEN

- I AM BLESSED AND HIGHLY FAVORED

- I AM HEALED

- I AM HEALTHY

- I AM HAPPY

- I AM MORE THAN A CONQUER

- I AM VICTORIOUS

- I AM STRONG

- I AM DELIVERED

- I AM AN HEIR OF THE WORLD

- I AM SUCCUESSFUL

- I AM THE HEAD AND NOT THE TAIL

- I AM ABOVE AND NOT BENEATH

- I AM GOD'S MASTERPIECE

- I AM A ROYAL PRIESTHOOD

- I AM MADE IN THE IMAGE OF GOD

- Whatever you're saying, you're inviting into your life.

- Your giving permission to enter your life.

- You're giving it access to your life.